DEADLY PREDATORS

Published by Hinkler Pty Ltd
45–55 Fairchild Street
Heatherton Victoria 3202 Australia
www.hinkler.com

© 2016 QEB Publishing, Inc.
Cover Design: Hinkler Studio

All rights reserved. No part of this publication may be reproduced, stored in a retrieval system, or transmitted in any way or by any means, electronic, mechanical, photocopying, recording or otherwise, without the prior written permission of Hinkler Pty Ltd.

ISBN: 978 1 4889 5227 2

Printed and bound in China

DEADLY PREDATORS

CAMILLA DE LA BÉDOYÈRE

CONTENTS

SHARKS AND OTHER OCEAN CREATURES 6
- BASKING SHARK 8
- LONGNOSE SAWSHARK 10
- LEMON SHARK 12
- EGGS AND PUPS 14
- GRAY REEF SHARK 16
- HAMMERHEAD SHARK 18
- TIGER SHARK 20
- SKELETONS AND SCALES 22
- ON THE MOVE 24
- BULL SHARK 26
- SHARKS AND PEOPLE 28
- DEADLY SHARKS 30
- GREAT WHITE SHARK 32
- GREAT WHITE SHARK 34
- PIRANHA 36
- BOX JELLYFISH 38
- ELECTRIC EEL 40

DANGEROUS REPTILES 42
- SEA SNAKE 44
- KING COBRA 46
- CORAL SNAKE 48
- ANACONDA 50
- RATTLESNAKE 52
- PUFF ADDER 54
- BLACK CAIMAN 56
- TAIPAN 58
- ALLIGATOR 60
- ALLIGATOR 62
- SALTWATER CROCODILE 64
- GILA MONSTER 66
- KOMODO DRAGON 68
- ALLIGATOR SNAPPING TURTLE 70
- POISON DART FROG 72

UP CLOSE!

UP CLOSE!

MINI MONSTERS 74
- FUNNELWEB SPIDER 76
- BROWN RECLUSE SPIDER 78
- BIRD-EATING SPIDER 80
- BLACK WIDOW SPIDER 82
- ARMY ANT 84
- ARMY ANT 86
- JUMPER ANT 88
- KILLER BEE 90
- PARALYSIS TICK 92
- MOSQUITO 94
- ASSASSIN BUG 96
- SCORPION 98
- LONOMIA 100
- SCUTIGERA 102

DEADLY MAMMALS 104
- VAMPIRE BAT 106
- TASMANIAN DEVIL 108
- HONEY BADGER 110
- CHIMPANZEE 112
- TIGER 114
- TIGER 116
- LION 118
- WOLVERINE 120
- WOLF 122
- POLAR BEAR 124
- KILLER WHALE 126

KILLER BIRDS 128
- GOLDEN EAGLE 130
- SECRETARY BIRD 132
- VULTURE 134

TOP 20 DEADLY FACTS 136
GLOSSARY 138
INDEX 142
PICTURE CREDITS 144

UP CLOSE!

UP CLOSE!

Words in **bold** are explained in the glossary on page 138.

5

SHARKS
AND OTHER
OCEAN CREATURES

Some of the strangest and most terrifying creatures on planet Earth lurk in water. While deadly sharks may be the most prominent predators, a host of other dangers can be found swimming in our oceans, rivers, and lakes.

BASKING SHARK

The enormous mouth of a basking shark is large enough to hold a child. Fortunately, a basking shark has no interest in human **prey** because it only eats tiny **plankton**!

Killer Fact
Basking sharks often swim near the sea's surface, and can even leap out of the water!

The largest basking sharks weigh up to 21 tons, five times as much as an elephant.

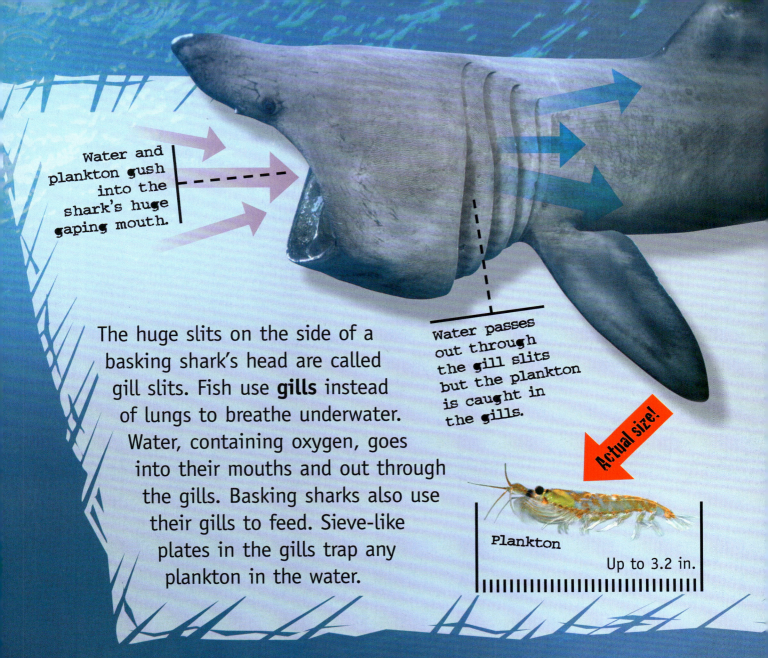

Water and plankton gush into the shark's huge gaping mouth.

Water passes out through the gill slits but the plankton is caught in the gills.

The huge slits on the side of a basking shark's head are called gill slits. Fish use **gills** instead of lungs to breathe underwater. Water, containing oxygen, goes into their mouths and out through the gills. Basking sharks also use their gills to feed. Sieve-like plates in the gills trap any plankton in the water.

Actual size!

Plankton

Up to 3.2 in.

Mystery Shark

Sharks are mysterious creatures, and scientists need to find out much more about their lifestyles. It is known that basking sharks go on long journeys in spring and summer, but no one knows for sure where they disappear to from November to March.

LONGNOSE SAWSHARK

This small shark has a peculiar snout that makes up more than one quarter of its whole body length. The shark uses its strange nose, called a rostrum, as a lethal weapon and to detect prey.

The sides of the long nose are lined with rows of teeth.

Up to 17.6 in.

Sawsharks have a small, flat body because they live on the seabed, where they hunt for small fish, squid, and shrimp. Their long noses are called saws and are lined with long, sharp teeth. Long feelers on the saw, called barbels, are used for touch. They also have teeth in their jaws, which they use for biting.

As they cruise along the seabed, sawsharks use their barbels to detect prey hidden in the sand and mud.

Killer Fact
Sawsharks sense electricity using organs called ampullae of Lorenzini. These are small, gel-filled holes in their saws.

Electric Sense

These sharks use their saws to swipe at their prey, or to rake through mud and find animals hiding. Their saws have another great use too—they can detect electricity. All animals use electricity to make their muscles work, and sharks have a super-sense that helps them to detect this electricity from other creatures.

LEMON SHARK

Lemon sharks are large coastal sharks. They prefer to live in warm, shallow waters near land, especially during the day. At night they swim to deeper water.

Lemon sharks have a wide, flat head.

Lemon sharks have small eyes and poor eyesight. The coastal waters where they live are often cloudy, so eyesight is not a great help in finding prey. Instead, these fish have special magnetic **sensors** in their snouts, which help them to find fish and shelled animals on the seabed.

Sharksuckers

Remoras, or sharksuckers, are long, thin fish with a special ability. They have suckers on the tops of their heads, which they use to stick to a shark or other large fish and hitch a ride. They feed off any scraps that the shark does not eat.

Killer Fact

Lemon sharks get their name from the yellow-brown color of their skin.

EGGS AND PUPS

Most fish lay eggs that **hatch** into baby fish. Sharks are special, though. Many of them don't lay eggs; they give birth to their young instead. Young sharks are called **pups**.

Lemon sharks can give birth to as many as 17 pups in a single year.

Most mother sharks keep their pups inside their bodies while they grow, to protect the pups from **predators** for as long as possible. When the pups are born they are able to swim away. Sharks don't look after their pups.

Mermaid's Purse

Sharks that do lay eggs, such as catsharks, lay the eggs in a thick, rubbery case called a mermaid's purse. These egg cases often have curly strings, which attach them to rocks or seaweed to stop them from floating away. The shark pups grow inside for up to ten months.

Up to 3.2 in.

Actual size!

This newborn lemon shark pup swims away from its mother.

KILLER FACT

Pups growing inside their mother may eat each other before they are even born. Sometimes only one or two pups survive.

GRAY REEF SHARK

Sometimes divers and snorkelers come face-to-face with one of the world's most threatening sharks—the gray reef shark. These hunters patrol coral reefs in groups.

KILLER FACT

Gray reef sharks patrol their own areas, and may attack swimmers and divers that come too close.

Most sharks are **solitary** animals. Gray reef sharks, however, often swim in groups in quiet spots during the day. At night they go their separate ways to hunt. When a gray reef shark is feeling threatened, it raises its snout, arches its back, and swims with a swaying motion. This menacing behavior warns enemies to move away—or prepare to be attacked.

Fishy Feasts

Gray reef sharks feed on squid, octopus, and shelled animals such as shrimp and lobsters. They also prey on the colorful fish that live among the reefs, such as these beautiful butterfly fish.

HAMMERHEAD SHARK

There are about 400 different types, or **species**, of shark, and some of the strangest-looking ones are called hammerheads. Like its relatives—such as the mallethead sharks—the great hammerhead has an extraordinary appearance.

A hammerhead's nostrils are far apart, helping it to sense the direction of different smells.

The huge, wide hammerhead's head has eyes positioned at the very ends. This shape probably helps the predator to move through water and change direction. The position of its eyes helps the shark to find its prey more easily, and work out how far away it is.

Fight for Life

Hammerheads can live for about 30 years, but few reach that great age. They are endangered, which means that they are at risk of becoming **extinct** because too many have been fished from the sea. They are also **cannibals**, and adults often prey on young hammerheads.

Killer Fact

Hammerheads like to feast on venomous stingrays, and can even eat the **venom-filled tails!**

TIGER SHARK

Meet the terrifying tiger shark—one of the most dangerous sharks in the world. These predators have been compared to garbage cans because they will try to eat almost anything.

They are called tiger sharks because their skin is marked with dark stripes and spots.

KILLER FACT

Tiger shark teeth are serrated, like a saw. As the sharks bite, they pull their heads from side to side and saw the flesh.

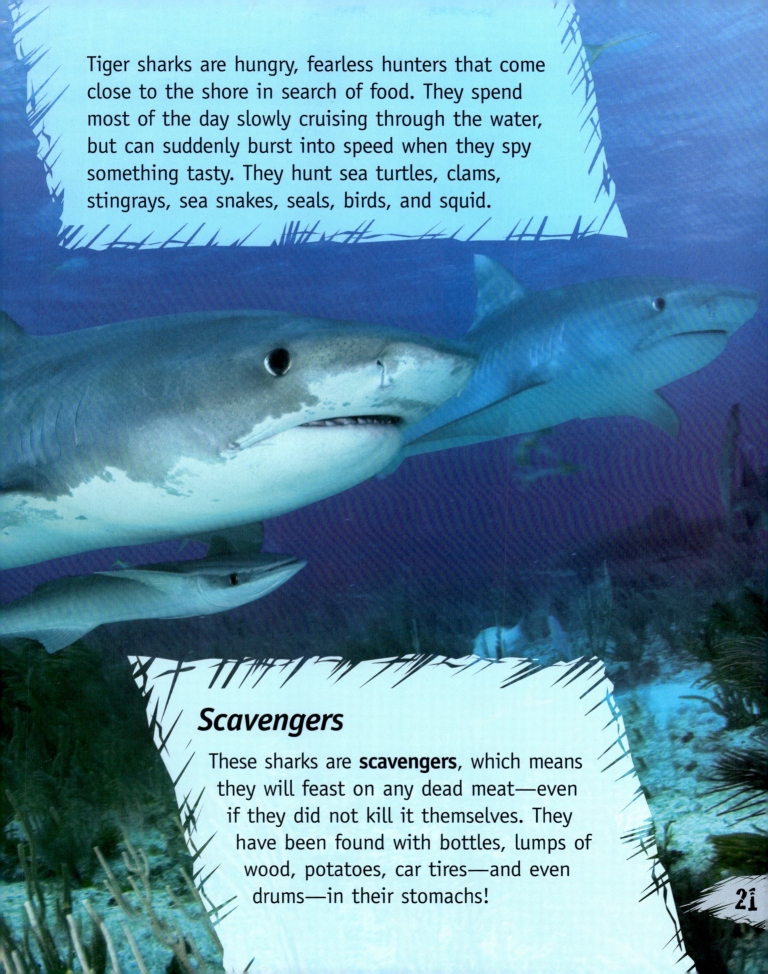

Tiger sharks are hungry, fearless hunters that come close to the shore in search of food. They spend most of the day slowly cruising through the water, but can suddenly burst into speed when they spy something tasty. They hunt sea turtles, clams, stingrays, sea snakes, seals, birds, and squid.

Scavengers

These sharks are **scavengers**, which means they will feast on any dead meat—even if they did not kill it themselves. They have been found with bottles, lumps of wood, potatoes, car tires—and even drums—in their stomachs!

SKELETONS AND SCALES

Most fish have a bony skeleton that gives their bodies shape, power, and strength. Sharks, however, don't have bones. Instead, their skeletons are made from a strong, bendy material called **cartilage**.

KILLER FACT

It isn't just shark teeth that can hurt—their skin can too. Its rough surface can tear the skin from a swimmer's leg.

Shark denticles

This swell shark has a spotted pattern to help it hide against the seabed.

Shark skin is covered with scales that are coated with enamel—the same tough material that makes our teeth hard. These scales are called **denticles**. Denticles help water to move smoothly over a shark, so it can swim fast.

Colors and Patterns

Some sharks have interesting patterns. Colors and patterns can help a shark to stay hidden from view. This is called **camouflage**. This wobbegong shark's strange shape and frilled mouth make a good disguise.

ON THE MOVE

A pointed nose and a streamlined body help a shark to swim fast.

Moving through water is harder work than moving through air. Most fish have a **streamlined** body shape, which means their bodies move through water easily. The fastest swimmers usually have a long, slender shape.

The world's fastest shark is the shortfin mako, which may reach speeds of 53 miles per hour—that's about the same speed as a cheetah chasing its prey.

Pectoral fins control direction and movements up and down.

The dorsal fin helps the fish to swim in S-shaped curves and stops it from rolling over.

The caudal, or tail, fin helps propel the shark through water.

KILLER FACT

Sharks have big, oily livers that help them to float, but if they stop swimming they sink to the seabed.

Slow Movers

Some sharks prefer life in the slow lane. They live on the seabed and move by swimming and almost "walking" with their fins. This leopard catshark roams the sandy seabed at night, searching for shellfish and small fish.

BULL SHARK

This broad, strong shark is known for its aggressive nature. Bull sharks are described as "short tempered," which means they are always ready for a fight!

Almost all sharks live in seas and oceans, where the water is salty. Bull sharks are more adaptable. They live in shallow coastal waters, but they also swim up rivers, and have even been found in **freshwater** lakes. Spotting a bull shark can be difficult, because they often swim in cloudy water.

Bull sharks usually live and hunt on their own.

KILLER FACT

Some experts believe that the bull shark is the deadliest shark in the world.

Lateral line

Sensitive Senses

Bull sharks have poor eyesight. Instead, they rely on a superb sense of smell. Like other sharks, they have a sensitive line that runs along their bodies, called the lateral line. This detects movement and vibrations in the water.

SHARKS AND PEOPLE

Humans are much more deadly than sharks. It is rare for sharks to attack people, and most human victims do survive an attack. People, however, kill up to 120 million sharks every year.

Many of these majestic marine predators are now in grave danger of becoming extinct. That means they will disappear from our planet forever. Sharks are fished for their meat and their fins, which are used in soup. They are also caught accidentally by fishermen.

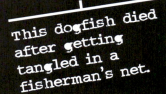

This dogfish died after getting tangled in a fisherman's net.

Shark cages allow scientists to study sharks close-up, without either the divers or the sharks being in danger.

Saving Sharks

We need sharks in our seas. They are part of the ocean ecosystem, and they play an important part in keeping the oceans healthy and in balance. We can help by not buying shark products, and by learning as much as we can about these beautiful fish.

Killer Fact

Worldwide numbers of sharks have plummeted since the 1950s because of fishing and pollution.

DEADLY SHARKS

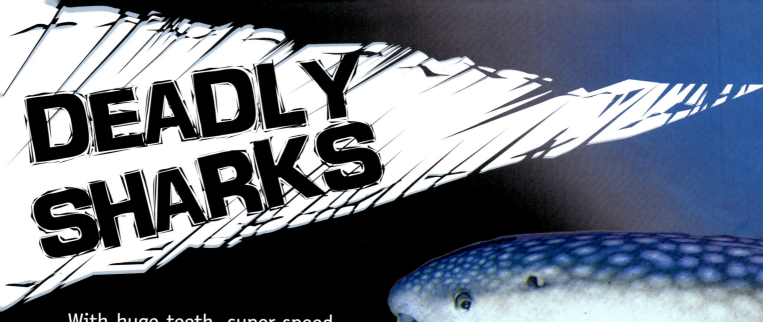

With huge teeth, super speed, and cold, dead eyes, sharks are among the world's most impressive predators.

Most sharks are long and thin, but they come in all shapes and sizes. The largest fish in the world is the mighty whale shark. It is harmless to people because it feeds on tiny animals called plankton.

Whale sharks are the giants of the ocean and grow to about 36 feet in length.

Frilled sharks have long, thin bodies and live deep underwater.

KILLER FACT

Sharks have been around for 400 million years, and had few predators—until humans began to hunt them.

All sharks are fish. They eat other animals, such as fish and squid. Sometimes, sharks mistake humans for food and attack them. Most sharks are wary of humans, and try to avoid them. Some sharks, however, are more aggressive.

This blue shark has a pointed nose, or snout, and large eyes so that it can see well in deep water.

GREAT WHITE SHARK

Does the great white shark really deserve to be called the oceans' most vicious predator? It is certainly well equipped to hunt, catch, and kill its prey.

A great white's bite is three times more powerful than a lion's bite.

Great whites are special sharks. They are big and powerful, they swim at speed and over great distances, and they are extremely skilled hunters. They can detect a single drop of blood in nearby water.

TURN THE PAGE TO GET UP-CLOSE TO A **DEADLY** GREAT WHITE SHARK

Great whites have 50–60 large teeth that are arranged in rows. Any tooth that falls out is quickly replaced.

Great whites usually swim alone, but are sometimes seen hunting in pairs or small groups.

Bite and Shake

When a great white takes a bite of its prey, it shakes its head from side to side. As it does so, the large triangular teeth saw through prey, cutting off large pieces of meat.

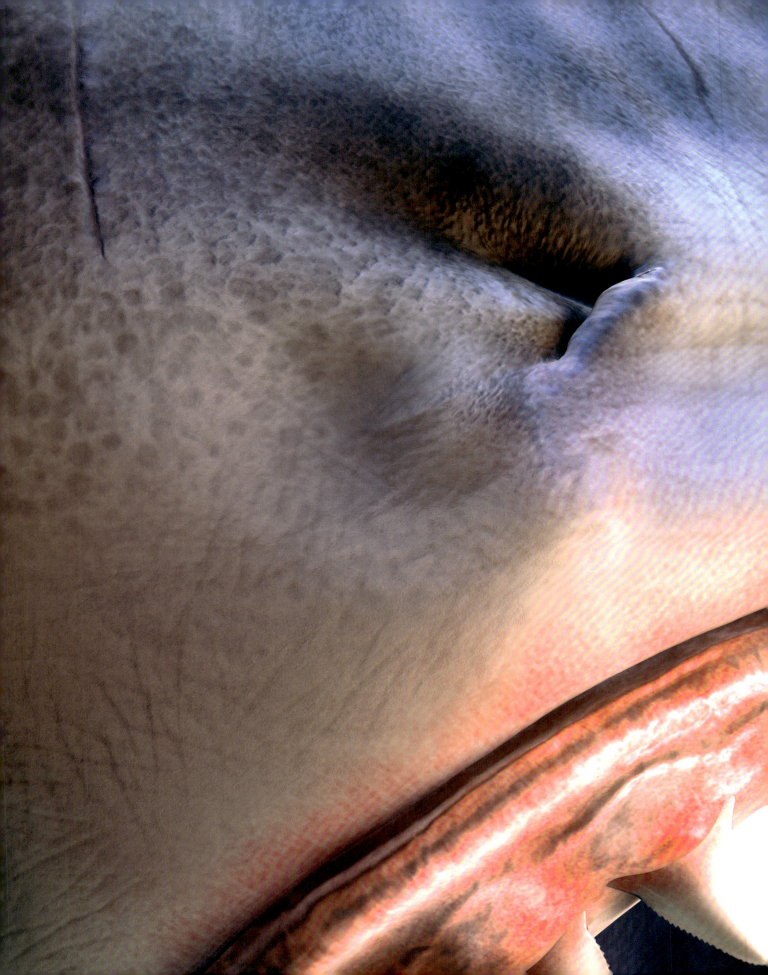

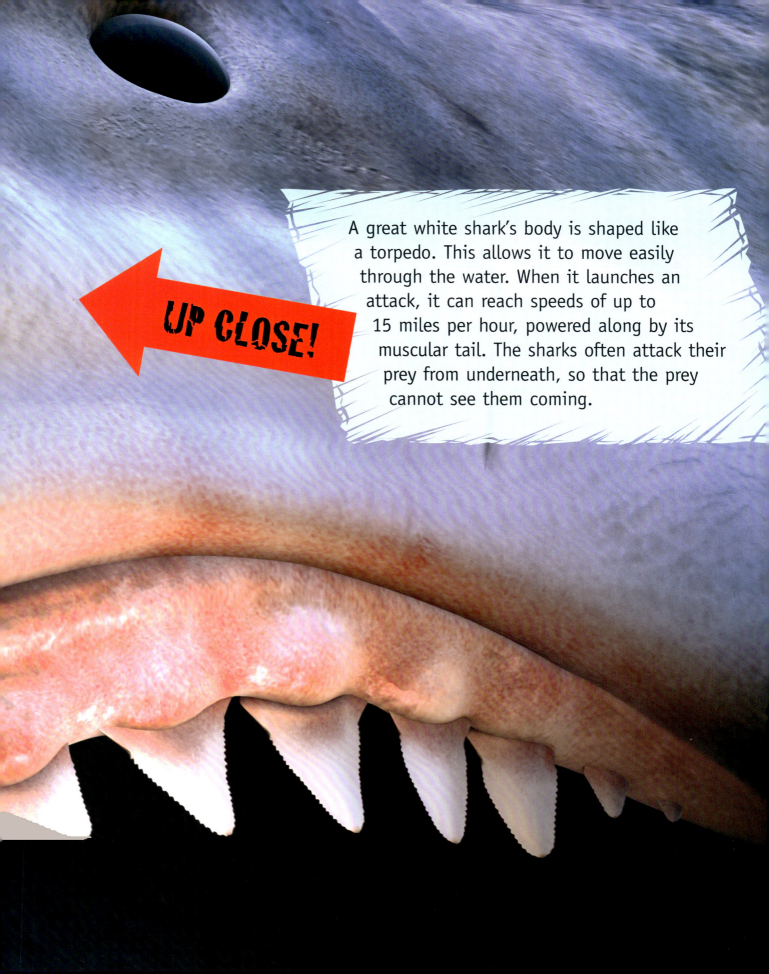

UP CLOSE!

A great white shark's body is shaped like a torpedo. This allows it to move easily through the water. When it launches an attack, it can reach speeds of up to 15 miles per hour, powered along by its muscular tail. The sharks often attack their prey from underneath, so that the prey cannot see them coming.

PIRANHA

It is said that a group of piranhas can strip the body of a cow to the bones in minutes. The truth is nowhere near as frightening! These fish do live in large groups called shoals, but they mostly feed on bugs, small fish, and shrimps.

Piranha teeth are pointed and razor-sharp.

Actual size!

Slice and Slash

Piranhas are able to devour flesh easily, because their strong jaws are lined with large, triangular teeth that interlock perfectly to make a cutting machine that can slash and slice.

KILLER FACT

People who have been bitten by piranhas have had entire fingers or toes cleanly sliced off!

Piranhas feed at dawn and dusk, when there is little sunlight and they can hide behind water plants, often in groups of up to 30 fish. Most piranhas attack prey alone.

Occasionally, a number of shoals may gather together into a much larger group to attack and feast on a large animal. However, this is very rare and probably only happens when there is a shortage of food.

BOX JELLYFISH

This is the most dangerous jellyfish in the world, and one of the most deadly creatures on planet Earth. There are a number of species of box jellyfish, all of which can be poisonous. The sea wasp box jellyfish is said to be the most toxic variety.

Venomous Jellies

This translucent sea-dweller may not look dangerous, but box jellyfish are deadly to many different animals, not least, humans. A sting from one of these creatures will cause serious harm and can often be fatal.

Sting in the Tail

On each tentacle there are around half a million microscopic darts, full of venom. When a jellyfish touches another animal or person the dart sticks in their skin and fires off venom. The sea turtle is the box jellyfish's only predator—the venom cannot get through the turtle's thick skin.

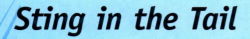

Box jellyfish have up to 15 tentacles, which may extend up to 10 ft in length.

A Caribbean box jellyfish with a fish in its stomach.

KILLER FACT

Box jellyfish can swim and actively hunt their prey, traveling at speeds of up to four knots through the water.

Box jellyfish swim in a school.

ELECTRIC EEL

Not all predators rely on jaws and claws to catch their prey. Electric eels are fish that **stun** and kill their prey in the most shocking way!

These fish live in the dark, murky waters of the Amazon River, where finding food is a challenge. Electric eels don't have good eyesight. Instead, they use weak electric pulses to find their way, like a **radar** system.

An electric eel also has electric organs along the length of its body. These are used to produce sudden electric shocks that stun the eel's prey or any predators that come too close.

KILLER FACT

Electric eels may be fish, but they breathe air—like us. They often have to come to the river's surface to gulp air.

The shock from an electric eel is strong enough to knock a horse off its feet.

Sit and Wait

Moray eels lurk in dark places and wait for food to swim by. They have two sets of jaws to grab their prey and drag it down into their throats. Some morays also have **toxins** on their skins.

Moray eels have large teeth, which they use to tear the flesh of their prey.

DANGEROUS REPTILES

Scales, spikes and terrifying teeth! It's no surprise that certain species of reptile have earned a reputation as some of the animal kingdom's most ferocious predators. Whether they lurk on land or catch their prey in water, they have been striking fear into both animals and humans for millions of years.

SEA SNAKE

KILLER FACT
Sea snakes are known for their mild tempers, and it is very difficult to make one angry enough to bite.

Sea snakes are venomous snakes that have taken to living and hunting underwater. Some sea snakes give birth to live baby snakes in water, while others come onto land to lay their eggs. They all have to come to the surface to breathe.

Sea snakes have more powerful venom than any other snakes, but they rarely bite people and have small **fangs**. Sea snakes feed on small fish and mollusks.

If they do bite, sea snakes inject only a tiny amount of venom and their victims may not even know they have been bitten at first. The venom causes muscles to break down, and death can occur in a few hours.

Sea snakes swim slowly along the ocean floor looking for prey.

Land and Sea

Sea snakes called kraits come ashore to **shed** their old skins, to mate, and to lay their eggs. The females lay three to ten eggs in old burrows left by seabirds or under rocks.

Like all snakes, kraits live alone, only coming together to mate.

KING COBRA

A king cobra puffs out its hood when threatened to make itself look bigger.

The king cobra is the longest of all venomous snakes, and can reach a length of more than 16 feet. It's so big that it can raise enough of its body off the ground to look a human in the eye!

As hunters, king cobras have powerful venom and size on their side, but they prey on other snakes, not people. When they are scared, these snakes rear up, spread out their hoods, and hiss. Putting on this scary show is a type of defense and it should make most enemies think twice before coming any closer.

KILLER FACT
King cobras rarely kill people, but Indian cobras attack at least 10,000 people every year in India alone.

Mamba!

Everyone in Africa knows to look out for this snake, which is one of the world's most dangerous predators. Mambas can slither faster than a person can run, are active during daytime, and have a deadly bite. Thankfully, mambas normally hunt birds and small animals—not people.

One bite from a mamba can kill an adult human in minutes.

Actual size!

CORAL SNAKE

Look at the two snakes shown on these pages. Can you tell the difference? The coral snake in the main picture has red and yellow bands that warn predators of its venomous bite, but the milk snake below is a harmless copycat.

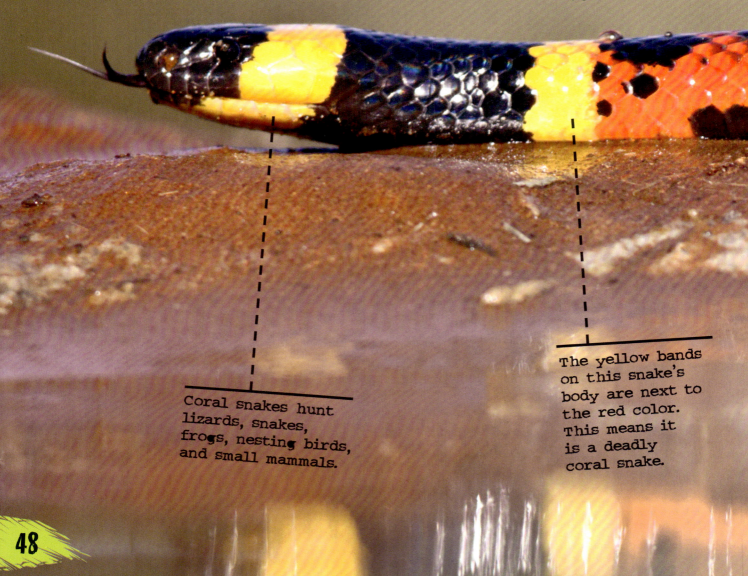

Coral snakes hunt lizards, snakes, frogs, nesting birds, and small mammals.

The yellow bands on this snake's body are next to the red color. This means it is a deadly coral snake.

KILLER FACT
Coral snake venom stops nerves and muscles from working. **Antivenoms** often save lives.

There are about 40 different types of coral snake, with different patterns of colored bands. Most live in burrows and only come out at night, so humans rarely encounter these venomous creatures.

Coral snakes need to keep jabbing at a victim to inject all their venom, so although the venom is deadly in large amounts, it is rare for people to die following an attack.

Smart Mimic

Milk snakes can bite, but they don't have venom. Their cunning disguise, however, makes them look like venomous coral snakes so predators stay away. A rhyme helps identify some of these colorful snakes: *If red touches yellow, it can kill a fellow, if red touches black, it's a friend of Jack.*

ANACONDA

Some fearsome reptiles take life at a slow pace, only stirring into action when hunger strikes. The **constrictor** snake may survive for several months on one big meal!

Pythons and boas don't use deadly venom to kill their prey—they squeeze them to death instead. Anacondas are a type of boa. They spend most of their lives in water, but slither onto land to hunt. They **ambush** animals that come to the water to drink, grabbing them in their coils.

Anacondas wrap themselves around their prey and squeeze until it **suffocates**.

Killer Fact
Anacondas don't lay eggs. They give birth to up to 80 young snakes at a time.

A large anaconda is heavier than an adult human.

Massive Monsters

Anacondas are big enough to prey on large animals, including caimans, deer, and even people. A record-breaking anaconda measured 27.7 feet long—as long as the net on a tennis court—and 43 inches around its middle.

RATTLESNAKE

If you hear the distinctive noise of a rattlesnake shaking its tail, you know it's time to escape—fast! These are supreme hunting serpents with speed, strength, and some unbelievable super skills.

Actual size!

The snake's rattle is at the end of its tail.

Rattlesnakes spend most of the day sunbathing, or hiding under rocks and in burrows. They hunt at dusk, when small mammals come out to find food, and can strike with amazing speed.

KILLER FACT
The Western diamondback is the most dangerous of all rattlesnakes. Its bite can prove deadly to humans.

When a snake flicks its tongue, it is smelling and tasting the air. When the snake pulls its tongue back into its mouth, it senses the smell using a special organ in the roof of its mouth.

Seeing in the Dark

Rattlesnakes can hunt in total darkness. They use special heat-detecting pits to find small animals. This super sense helps the snake to build up a picture of where an animal is, its size, shape, and even its movements.

Heat-detecting pit

53

PUFF ADDER

The body is thick, with a girth of up to 16 in.

When a puff adder is feeling scared, it puffs out its body to make itself look larger and hisses. But this snake has little to fear from anyone—it is one of Africa's deadliest snakes.

KILLER FACT
Puff adders are responsible for nearly two-thirds of all snakebites in Africa.

Puff adders are the most common snakes in Africa, and often live close to humans. They kill more people in Africa than any other kind of snake.

The pattern on its skin keeps the snake well hidden.

Hiding

With brown and cream camouflage, puff adders hide in the undergrowth, ready to ambush small animals. Their large bodies slither silently, but when prey is close, these heavy snakes turn into speedy hunters. If they meet a human, puff adders can easily deliver enough venom to kill.

A puff adder's long fangs can pierce leather!

BLACK CAIMAN

Caimans are members of the crocodile and alligator family. Although they are great predators themselves, some types of caiman are close to extinction because humans hunt them for their skins.

Killer Fact
Caimans attack people for three main reasons: to eat, to defend their homes, or to defend their young.

Caimans use their excellent eyesight and sense of smell to hunt fish, waterbirds, and turtles. They spend most of the day floating in water, but when they come ashore at night, they may hunt mammals, especially **capybaras**, dogs, pigs, and deer. They have been known to attack people.

When caimans are underwater, special flaps close over their nostrils and ears to stop water from getting in.

The black caiman is the largest predator in the Amazon rainforest.

Head is 2–3 in. long

Actual size!

Caring Mother

Female black caimans lay up to 60 eggs in a nest near slow-flowing water. They stay on their nests to protect their eggs from predators, and take care of the babies after they hatch.

TAIPAN

The deadly taipan lives in Australian deserts, and is the most venomous snake in the world. Taipans belong to a group of snakes that are called elapids.

Killer Fact
A taipan has enough venom to kill 250,000 mice, 150,000 rats—or 100 people!

The taipan is also called the "fierce snake."

Like most snakes, taipans hunt small animals to eat, even entering their burrows. They only attack people if they are feeling scared.

A Quick Death

Most elapids are fast-moving snakes that can strike with lightning speed. When elapid snakes bite their prey, venom runs down grooves on each fang's surface or through a canal in the center of the fang. The venom usually affects the victim's **nervous system**, so it cannot move or breathe.

Taipans have needle-like fangs at the fronts of their mouths.

ALLIGATOR

American alligators were so heavily hunted by humans for their skins that they were in danger of dying out completely. Today, these impressive predators are protected.

Killer Fact
Although they breathe air, alligators can stay underwater for up to six hours at a time.

This alligator is hiding under the algae, waiting for unsuspecting prey to pass by.

Like other reptiles, alligators need to keep warm to move at speed, so they spend most of the day floating, and **basking** in the sun. When they float, alligators can stay almost motionless. Just their eyes and the tips of their noses poke above the water—looking for prey.

TURN THE PAGE TO GET UP-CLOSE TO A **DEADLY** ALLIGATOR!

Smaller young alligators often gather together in large groups.

Baby alligators are just 8.7 in long when they hatch.

Actual size!

Taking Care

Female alligators build huge nests and lay about 45 eggs at a time. After the baby alligators hatch, their mother carefully lifts them in her mouth and takes each one down to the water.

UP CLOSE!

Powerful muscles snap an alligator's jaws shut tight when it bites its prey. However, the muscles that open the jaws are much weaker, and an adult human is strong enough to hold an alligator's jaws shut.

Alligators usually eat smaller prey that they can kill in one bite, such as fish or turtles, but they will also attack larger animals, such as deer or dogs.

SALTWATER CROCODILE

When the world's largest reptile decides it is hungry, no one is safe. The saltwater crocodile, or "saltie," is a fearsome hunter that uses **stealth**, speed, and strength to kill.

Salties have 64–68 pointed teeth in their long jaws.

Saltwater crocodiles live in warm waters in Asia and the Pacific Ocean. These massive crocodilians can grow to at least 16 feet long, but it is thought that some males may grow to more than 23 feet from snout to tail-tip. Despite their huge and heavy bodies, crocodiles can move with great speed on land and can outrun a human.

Salties hunt fish, mammals, and birds. They clamp their jaws around their prey, and sink below the water. Then the crocodiles begin the "death roll," spinning their bodies until the prey is drowned.

Actual size!

3.3 in.

Death Roll

Crocodiles can bite, but they can't chew. Their piercing teeth are perfect for grabbing hold of prey, but this might not kill it. That's why crocodiles perform a death roll.

Killer Fact
Crocodiles sometimes hunt in groups, which suggests they are smarter than most reptiles.

GILA MONSTER

Gila monsters move slowly, so they pose very little risk to humans.

These lizards are called monsters for a good reason—they have venomous bites. Gila monsters mostly use their venom to defend themselves from other animals.

Gilas are slow-moving desert lizards that prey on birds' eggs and bugs. Like other reptiles, these lizards can use their tongues to sense if food is around. When they flick their tongues, they are "tasting" the air.

Big Digger

The Mexican beaded lizard also has a venomous bite. It uses its large claws to dig burrows, where it hides. Its venom subdues its prey, such as birds and small mammals. Its bite is believed to be harmless to humans.

Many venomous animals prefer to warn their enemies away, rather than fight them. Gila monsters have black bodies with bold patterns of pink, yellow, or orange. These colors warn predators that the lizards are venomous.

Killer Fact
Some people keep Gila monsters as pets, which is a bad idea. Eight people have died from Gila bites.

KOMODO DRAGON

KILLER FACT
Komodo Island has become a huge wildlife park where the dragons are protected.

Few predators are more fascinating than the Komodo dragon. These huge reptiles rule the island of Komodo in Indonesia, but there are fewer than 5,000 of them left in the wild.

Komodos were not discovered until about 100 years ago.

Komodos are the world's heaviest lizards, and a male can weigh more than an adult human. They have strength rather than speed, and lie in wait for passing prey, to ambush it. Komodos aren't fussy and will eat almost anything they find, including deer, pigs—and even humans!

Deadly Bite

When a Komodo spots its prey, it springs to action and uses its sharp claws to hold down the animal. A quick bite with its sharp teeth allows the Komodo to pass venom into the prey's body. The injured animal runs away, but will soon weaken from its wound. The Komodo can then stroll over and finish its meal.

One side of a Komodo's teeth has jagged **serrations**.

ALLIGATOR SNAPPING TURTLE

This reptilian predator lurks in murky swamps. When it lifts its ugly, scaly head above the water, the bad-tempered animal snaps its jaws like a prehistoric monster.

Alligator snapping turtles have one of the nastiest bites around. They grow large and heavy, and live in freshwater where they feed on fish. Snapping turtles can reach the age of 100 or more.

With their spiked shells, these reptiles are known as the dinosaurs of the turtle world.

Not What It Seems!

When a fish approaches a little red, wriggling worm, it has no idea it is swimming into the jaws of death. For that is no worm, but a lure—a worm-like lump of flesh inside the turtle's mouth that tempts fish and frogs to come close—SNAP!

Killer Fact

When the turtle sees food, it fills its lure with blood so that it looks red, plump, and very tasty!

POISON DART FROG

KILLER FACT
The two-inch-long golden poison dart frog has enough venom to kill ten grown men!

At just a couple of inches long, the brightly colored poison dart frog packs a powerful punch. A pinhead's worth of its poison, **batrachotoxin**, can stop the heart of a large mammal or 20,000 mice. What's more, the poison is located on the surface of the skin, making this predator deadly to the touch.

Poison dart frogs live in the lush rainforests of Central and South America, and can also be found on a few Hawaiian islands.

Colors

There are more than 100 species of poison dart frog, whose colors and patterns vary. The black and green species has black spots, the strawberry or blue jeans frog is all red with blue legs, and the yellow-banded species is colored yellow and black. The frog's beautiful appearance serves as a poisonous warning to potential predators.

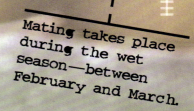

Mating takes place during the wet season—between February and March.

Deadly Diet

Poison dart frogs, also known as poison arrow frogs, are so called because some tribes used their secretions to poison their darts. Arrow frogs are not poisonous in captivity, as these frogs gain their poison through their diet—a particular arthropod and other insects they eat in the wild. In turn, these insects most likely obtain the poison from eating plants. The frogs' excellent vision allows them to spot prey on the forest floor, before reeling it in with their long sticky tongues.

The bright blue frog has a life span of around 5–7 years.

MINI MONSTERS

Insects make up around three-quarters of all animal species on Earth and play an important role in the food chain, serving as prey for larger animals. But many of these creatures are deadly predators in their own right—meet the small but mighty mini monsters.

FUNNELWEB SPIDER

Funnelweb spiders have glossy, brown, or black bodies, and do not look all that scary. But looks can be deceiving ...

A funnelweb spider waits in its tunnel for a tasty treat to pass by.

Hidden from View

Funnelweb spiders hide in dark, damp places. They live in burrows and weave silken trip lines around the entrances. When a little creature walks on the silk thread, the spider feels the vibrations and leaps out of its burrow to attack.

The venom affects the nervous systems of humans and monkeys, but not other mammals.

Of all funnelweb spiders, the most dangerous are male Sydney funnelweb spiders, which have such deadly venom they can kill their prey in seconds. They have fangs nearly 0.4 inches long.

When it is time to mate, male Sydney funnelweb spiders come out of their burrows to look for females. They search relentlessly, and attack anything that gets in their way.

KILLER FACT

Funnelweb spiders can't swim, but they can stay alive in water for up to 30 hours.

BROWN RECLUSE SPIDER

Brown recluse spiders may be small, but they are fanged, fast-moving, eight-legged predators.

The pedipalps are short limbs on either side of the head.

Brown recluse spiders use special legs, called pedipalps, to grab and hold their prey while they inject venom with their fangs. The bite of a brown recluse is usually painless to a human, but within a few hours a sore wound develops, which needs to be treated by a doctor.

KILLER FACT

Brown recluse spiders have a violin-shaped marking on their bodies, and are sometimes called violin spiders.

This spider's venom works by eating away at the skin, and can cause death in some cases.

Most spiders have eight eyes, but brown recluse spiders have six. They build large, sticky webs that look like silken sheets, and often make their homes in dark corners of houses. They use their webs to hold their egg sacs, rather than to catch prey. Instead, they hunt at night.

Each egg sac contains over 30,000 eggs.

BIRD-EATING SPIDER

This is no mini monster—it's a maxi monster! The goliath bird-eating spider is the heaviest spider in the world, and it attacks birds, lizards, and frogs.

All spiders have eight legs and a body that is divided into two parts. They can sense other animals through their legs, which are very sensitive to movement.

Goliath bird-eating spiders make a hissing noise to warn predators away. If that doesn't work, they rear up on their back legs and expose their fangs, ready to bite. They can also shoot irritating hairs at attackers.

Spiders use the hairs on their legs to sense the movements of other animals that are nearby.

KILLER FACT

Females can live for 20 years. Males rarely live for more than six years because they die after **mating**.

A Nasty Bite

The body of a goliath bird-eating spider can measure more than 4 inches and each fang is about 0.75 inches long. These spiders can inject venom when they bite.

BLACK WIDOW SPIDER

Black widow spiders are dangerous, but it's insects that have the most to fear from their venomous attacks. Black widows set traps and deliver lethal bites.

KILLER FACT
Occasionally, female black widows kill and eat males after mating with them.

The spiders add drops of glue to the threads of a web to make them more sticky.

Black widows build messy webs using special bristles on their legs. Once the victim is trapped in the web, a spider can inject it with venom up to 15 times stronger than a rattlesnake's.

Smart Moves

Most male spiders have to impress the females before mating. A male Australian redback spends more than an hour dancing for a female, but if she doesn't like his dance, she might eat him!

Black widows only bite people to defend themselves, and their bites are rarely fatal.

ARMY ANT

Few things can stop a horde of army ants when they go on a march. By working together, these insects are more powerful than many predators.

Huge jaws can cut and slice, breaking up victims' bodies into small pieces in minutes.

Killer Fact

One **colony** of army ants can kill up to 100,000 bugs in one day. Flies follow them around and eat any leftovers.

Strength in Numbers

Army ants are social insects that live and work in large groups called colonies. The ants have hooks on their legs, which help them to climb and stick together to make massive nests, called bivouacs, out of their own bodies.

The ants build a new nest out of their own bodies in a different place each day.

TURN THE PAGE TO GET UP-CLOSE TO A **DEADLY** ARMY ANT ATTACK

UP CLOSE!

One army ant can give a nasty bite, but when hundreds of thousands of them set out from their nest on a feeding frenzy, their impact is incredible.

Their usual prey includes scorpions, beetles, and spiders—but they devour almost anything in their paths, from cockroaches to birds and goats. They will even attack people.

JUMPER ANT

There are at least 10,000 species of ant in the world. Most ants can bite or sting—or make venomous droplets that inflict pain. Their venom is similar to that of bees.

KILLER FACT

Many people are allergic to the chemicals in these ants' stings, and can become seriously sick after one bite.

This jumper ant has managed to catch a bee in its jaws.

Bulldog and jumper ants are larger than most ants, and use their excellent eyesight to find other ants and bees to prey on. They are aggressive insects that will leap into action when they are threatened—and can actually jump at a victim!

Big Stingers

Little black bullet ants inflict the most painful of all ant stings. Fire ants use their stings to defend the large homes they make and share. They use their pincers to grab hold of their victims and just keep on stinging!

As jumper ants sink their large jaws into an animal or human, they use a stinger to inject powerful chemicals that cause great pain.

KILLER BEE

One bee on its own is unlikely to do much harm to a person. When a group of bees gets together, it's a different matter. A buzzing, angry swarm is terrifying—and dangerous.

Killer bees will chase an animal over longer distances than normal bees.

Fast Fighters

Killer bees are much more likely to attack than ordinary bees. They are quick to create huge angry swarms and can detect people 49 feet away from their nests.

KILLER FACT

Bees die after one sting. Wasps and hornets can keep stinging until they run out of venom.

Bees feed on nectar and pollen from flowers, and will only sting other animals or people to defend themselves. Most bees have a single sting with tiny hooks called barbs on it. The barbs help the sting to stay in the victim, while venom is pumped into the victim's body, causing pain and swelling.

The sting of a killer bee is no worse than any other bee. It is only a problem when an animal is stung lots of times.

PARALYSIS TICK

Ticks are insects with eight legs, like spiders, and a blood-sucking lifestyle. Most ticks cause little harm, but some of them carry a deadly secret.

These bugs are **parasites**, which means they feed on another animal while it is still alive. Ticks have sharp mouthparts that pierce a hole in a victim's flesh, and inject a liquid to stop blood from **clotting**. The ticks suck blood until their bodies are large and swollen, and then they fall to the ground.

KILLER FACT
Other ticks also cause disease. They carry **bacteria** that infect the wounds they make.

Actual sizes!
Before feeding
After feeding

Australian paralysis ticks have another nasty trick. They don't just suck blood—they inject a venom that causes the victim to become **paralyzed**. Without treatment, the victim may die.

Paralysis ticks prey on many kinds of animal, including pets and people.

Tick **larvae** have three pairs of legs, while adult ticks have four pairs.

Only a small number of tick eggs will actually hatch.

Monster Moms

Female ticks must feed on blood before they can lay eggs, and this is when they inject dangerous toxins. They lay up to 3,000 eggs at a time. Lazy males sometimes suck blood from the females!

MOSQUITO

At their best, mosquitoes are buzzing, biting bloodsuckers. At their worst, these flies are among the world's most dangerous pests.

Male mosquitoes mostly feed from flowers, but females have to feed on blood before they can lay their eggs. They search out mammals and birds to attack, piercing the skin with their long mouthparts.

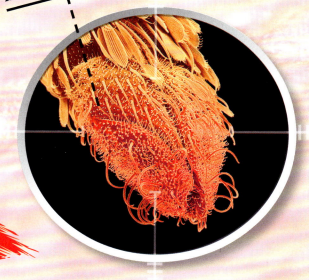

The tip of the mouthpart is needle-sharp.

As they break the skin, mosquitoes inject **saliva** to stop blood from clotting so they can keep sucking it up. Mosquitoes are parasites, and the animals they feed upon are called **hosts**.

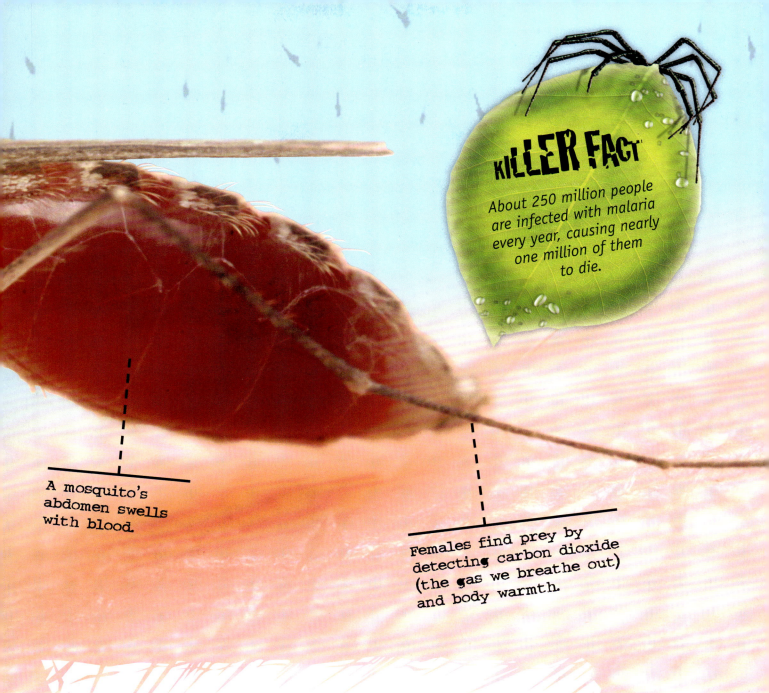

A mosquito's abdomen swells with blood.

Females find prey by detecting carbon dioxide (the gas we breathe out) and body warmth.

KILLER FACT
About 250 million people are infected with malaria every year, causing nearly one million of them to die.

Deadly Disease

Some mosquitoes, especially those that live in hot countries, carry bacteria that cause sickness. When the flies move from host to host, they pass on the bacteria, which can lead to deadly diseases such as malaria and dengue fever.

ASSASSIN BUG

Assassin bugs may be small, but they are definitely deadly. These blood-sucking beasts hunt prey using a variety of cunning tricks.

Assassin bugs hold on to prey using sticky pads on their front legs. Needle-like mouthparts pierce the victim's body and inject a toxic liquid that turns flesh into a tasty juice. A big cockroach takes just three seconds to die—and the bug then sucks up its liquid meal.

Some assassin bugs ambush their prey, or trick them by dangling dead insects outside their homes. Others pretend to be flies caught in a web, and pounce on the spider that comes to investigate.

The toxic saliva in the bite can cause blindness.

This assassin bug is attacking a termite worker.

An assassin bug's bite is one of the most painful insect bites in the world.

Kissing Bug

Kissing bugs are assassin bugs that prey on larger animals, such as mammals, birds, and people. They suck blood from their victims and pass on the deadly Chagas disease.

KILLER FACT

Chagas disease, spread by assassin bugs, kills about 50,000 people a year, and causes heart disease in many survivors.

SCORPION

The huge imperial scorpion has powerful pincers to kill its prey. Smaller, weaker scorpions rely on venomous stings to defeat their victims.

KILLER FACT

Death stalker scorpions are very aggressive, and can deliver lethal venom to humans.

The imperial scorpion holds the record as the world's largest scorpion.

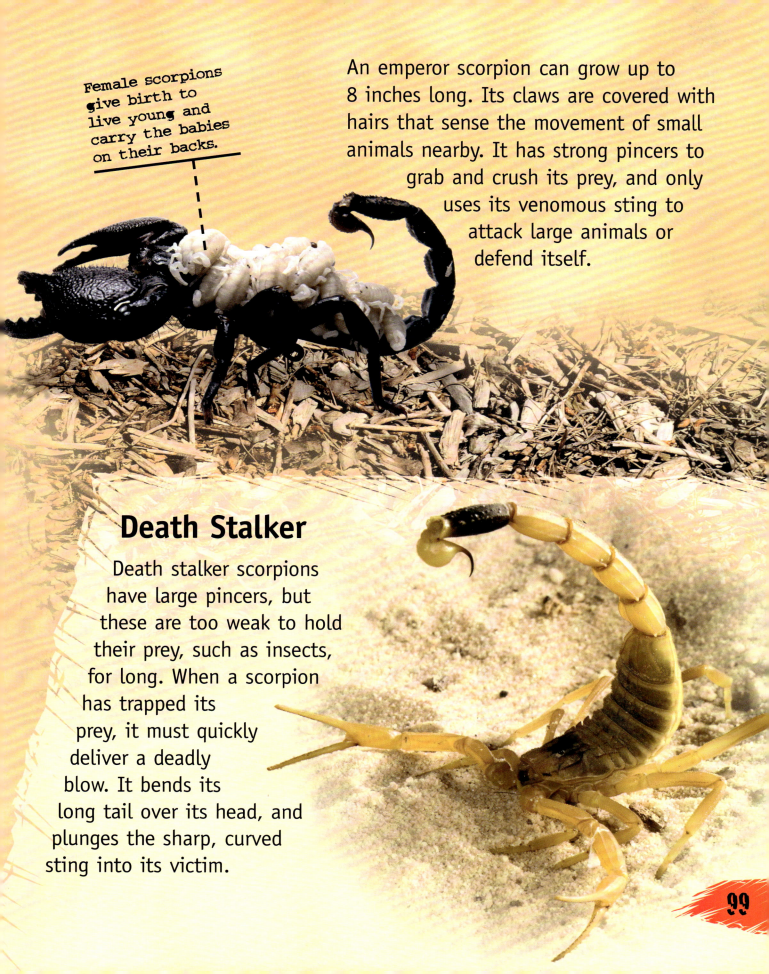

Female scorpions give birth to live young and carry the babies on their backs.

An emperor scorpion can grow up to 8 inches long. Its claws are covered with hairs that sense the movement of small animals nearby. It has strong pincers to grab and crush its prey, and only uses its venomous sting to attack large animals or defend itself.

Death Stalker

Death stalker scorpions have large pincers, but these are too weak to hold their prey, such as insects, for long. When a scorpion has trapped its prey, it must quickly deliver a deadly blow. It bends its long tail over its head, and plunges the sharp, curved sting into its victim.

LONOMIA

KILLER FACT
Scientists hope to be able to make life-saving medicine using lonomia venom.

A killer caterpillar's deadly spines send out a clear warning to predators—this creature will not make a tasty snack.

The colorful caterpillar becomes a brown moth.

A lonomia caterpillar will become a moth one day. While it is still young, however, a caterpillar's job is to eat and grow—and avoid being eaten itself.

Prickles and Poison

The sharp spines warn predators, such as birds, lizards, and frogs, that this soft-bodied mini monster is carrying a nasty venom. The spines break when they pierce a victim's skin, and the venom enters its body.

The bright colors help to warn predators.

If enough venom gets into a person's body, it can cause severe pain, bruising, and even death!

Most caterpillars are camouflaged. They are often green or brown so they can hide on plants. Lonomia caterpillars, however, are covered with sharp spines to put off predators!

SCUTIGERA

Creepy-crawlies, spiders, scorpions, and stinging bugs are some of the world's most incredible creatures. They belong to one enormous group of animals, called **invertebrates**.

Scutigera have well-developed eyes to help them spot their prey.

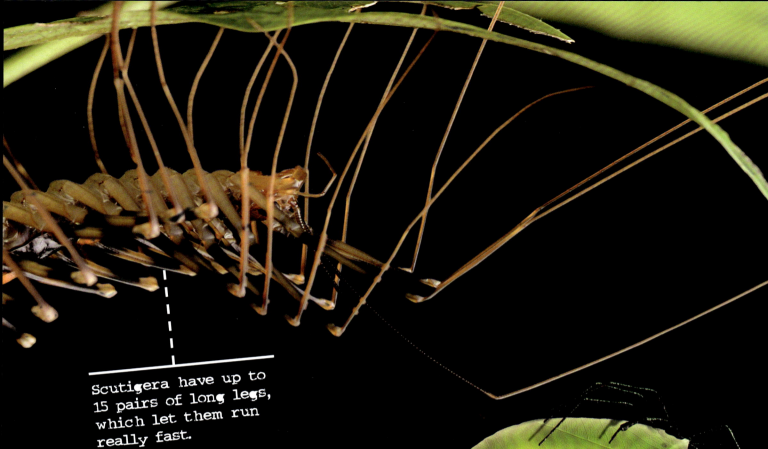

Scutigera have up to 15 pairs of long legs, which let them run really fast.

Invertebrates are usually small and have no bones, but many of them are still fearsome predators. This giant long-legged centipede is called a scutigera. Its body is divided into **segments**, and there are pairs of legs on most segments.

Claws on the first pair of legs inject a deadly venom into a victim. Scutigera eat other invertebrates, such as beetles.

KILLER FACT

The venom from some scutigera centipedes is strong enough to make a human very sick.

Creepy Legs

Why does any bug need 15 pairs of legs? They aren't just for running—these limbs do another important job. Scutigera use their legs to feel their way in the dark, and to find prey.

DEADLY MAMMALS

From winged beasts to sharp-toothed carnivores, deadly mammals come in all shapes and sizes.

These creatures may be warm-blooded, but they kill their prey in cold blood. Every one of these mammals is dangerous if encountered in the wild, so it pays to be cautious with these predators—cuddly appearances can deceive!

VAMPIRE BAT

There are few predators with a worse reputation than the little vampire bat. That's no wonder given their ugly faces, nasty "fangs," and a feeding habit of drinking blood.

Vampire bats sense warm bodies with their noses.

Killer Fact
Vampire bats have special heat-sensing areas on their noses that help them to find their prey.

Vampire bats can run at speeds of up to 5 miles per hour.

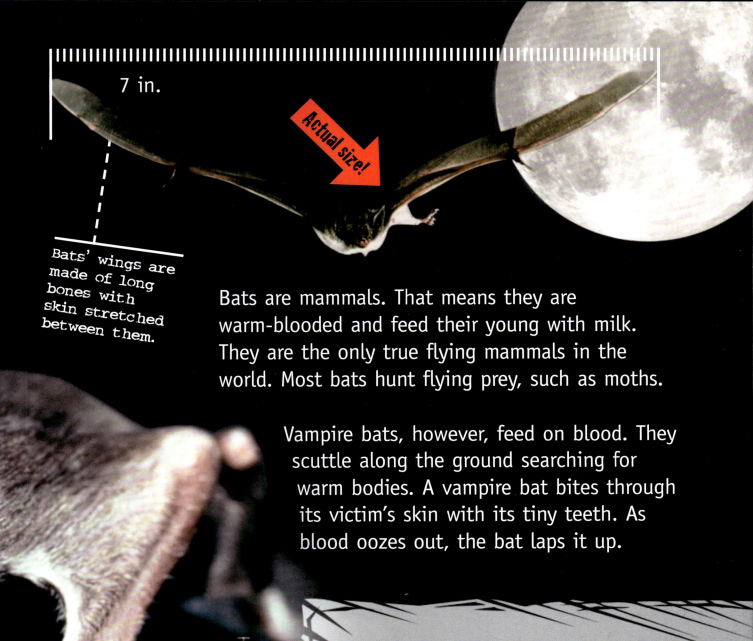

7 in.

Actual size!

Bats' wings are made of long bones with skin stretched between them.

Bats are mammals. That means they are warm-blooded and feed their young with milk. They are the only true flying mammals in the world. Most bats hunt flying prey, such as moths.

Vampire bats, however, feed on blood. They scuttle along the ground searching for warm bodies. A vampire bat bites through its victim's skin with its tiny teeth. As blood oozes out, the bat laps it up.

Pain-Free Feeding

A vampire bat's sharp teeth can tear through skin without the victim feeling a thing. The bats produce a chemical that reduces the pain. Grooves in their tongues help blood to pour into their throats.

TASMANIAN DEVIL

KILLER FACT
Tasmanian devils have pink ears, which turn red when they are very angry!

Tasmanian devils deserve their name—they are ferocious and extremely bad-tempered. Devils are famous for their blood-curdling nighttime screeches!

Flexible front feet allow devils to hold their food.

Food Fight

Tasmanian devils have a great sense of smell. If one devil is feeding, others detect the smell and rush to share the feast. Fights sometimes break out over food, but usually the hungry animals just growl at one another.

Devils can eat nearly half their own body weights in just 30 minutes.

Tasmanian devils look like small bears, but they are **marsupials** —a type of mammal that gives birth to tiny young that grow inside a pouch on their mother's body.

These predators survive on a diet of meat, which they get by killing animals, such as wallabies and possums, or by scavenging.

HONEY BADGER

The name honey badger may sound sweet, but these beasts are totally fearless predators. They instinctively strike and kill, and they are not fussy about what they attack.

KILLER FACT
Honey badgers can kill small crocodiles and pythons that are more than 10 feet long!

These predators explore every avenue to find food. They dig holes, searching for worms and bugs, climb trees to raid honey and grubs from bees' nests, and even scamper to high branches to steal eggs from raptor nests!

Badgers live alone and only come together once a year to breed.

It takes courage to face a lion devouring its prey head on, and then scare that lion away. But that's what honey badgers are willing to do when they have their sights set on lunch.

Thick skin around the neck and small ears protects the honey badger from injury in fights.

Best Friends

Honeyguide birds perch near to bees' nests, and show honey badgers where to dig or climb. Once the badger has opened a nest, the bird swoops in to feast on bees and beeswax.

CHIMPANZEE

Some animal experts think chimpanzees are among the most impressive of all predators. They are fast and clever, and work in gangs to track and kill other animals.

When they feel threatened, chimps bare their teeth.

Toolmakers

Like humans, chimps make tools to hunt with. They strip bark from a branch, sharpen it, and use it to kill small animals. Twigs are used to dig in termite nests.

KILLER FACT
Chimpanzees are our closest living relatives and some of the cleverest animals alive.

For a long time, scientists thought chimps enjoyed a diet of fruits, leaves, nuts, roots, and bugs. Then it was discovered they also prey on pigs and monkeys, and even kill chimps from other families.

These apes hunt cooperatively, which means they work together and have different jobs to do. One chimp might chase a monkey through the trees, while another blocks its escape route and a third waits to ambush it.

TIGER

Tigers are the largest of the big cats, and one of the largest of all predators. These majestic animals combine beauty, stealth, and speed with a deadly instinct to kill.

The Siberian tiger lives high in the mountains, where it hunts deer and small mammals.

A tiger's stripes camouflage it, keeping it hidden from its prey.

KILLER FACT
There used to be eight species of tiger, but three of them have become extinct in the last 60 years.

Most tigers live and hunt alone. They patrol their areas, which are called territories, looking for clues that other tigers or other animals are nearby. Tigers have a great sense of smell, which helps them to find prey hiding in the jungle.

TURN THE PAGE TO GET UP-CLOSE TO A **DEADLY** TIGER

Big Appetites

Tigers can attack large animals, such as pigs, deer, and monkeys. They may even hunt baby elephants and rhinoceroses. Once it has killed its prey, a tiger will **gorge** itself on meat, eating up to 88 pounds at one time. It may keep returning to the carcass to feed on it over the next few days.

Tigers hunt by stalking their prey, sneaking up close to attack with a short burst of speed. Tigers can leap up to 32 feet to pounce on prey. Their front legs pin their victims to the ground, while they bite the throat with their powerful jaws. Prey often escape, though, and only one in every 20 tiger hunts results in a kill.

UP CLOSE!

LION

Lions are unusual big cats. Like most predators, they have deadly weapons to catch and kill their prey. Unlike most predators, lions hunt in groups.

KILLER FACT
Lion hunts are most successful on moonless nights. In the dark, prey can't see the lions **stalking** them.

Even friendly, **tame** lions can suddenly turn on a human and decide it's time to eat!

Lions are strong and smart. They have superb senses of sight and smell, which help them to find antelope and zebras. They live and hunt in family groups called **prides**.

Lionesses do most of the hunting. They stalk their prey, until it is time for the kill. They share the meat with the pride. An adult male can eat up to 95 lb. at one time—the weight of a 13-year-old child!

canine tooth

Actual size!

2 in.

Reasons to Kill

Hunting for food is hard work, but it's worth the effort. Meat is packed with energy, so a predator only needs to eat occasionally. In contrast, animals that eat plants need to spend most of their time feeding to get enough energy to live.

WOLVERINE

These weasel-like animals are no bigger than a dog, but they are brave and fierce enough to attack a bear.

Wolverines live in the world's cold north, where food is scarce. They have long, thick fur to keep them warm.

These fearless predators are always on the move, and chase animals much bigger than themselves, such as deer. They leap boldly at their prey, grabbing them in their strong jaws.

Wolverines can kill prey that are many times bigger than they are.

A wolverine's jaws are as powerful as a crocodile's. They can crunch through the large bones of caribou.

Broad, furry paws help wolverines walk on icy surfaces.

KILLER FACT
Wolverines are not just predators. They also scavenge, which means they eat dead animals they find.

WOLF

Wolves often appear in fairy tales and legends as wily killers. They are certainly smart predators with a nose for danger.

During the winter, wolves grow thick, fluffy fur.

KILLER FACT
Gray wolves are the largest members of the dog family, and all of our pet dogs are descended from wolves.

The alpha female is the only female in the pack that gives birth to cubs.

Rare Beasts

Wolves once roamed large parts of the world, but they are now mostly found in northern forests. They live in groups called packs that are ruled by a top male and female called the **alpha pair**.

When prey is near, wolves give chase, running for hours. They work as a team, and may split up to attack from all sides.

Powerful jaws can crush bones.

Wolves keep in contact with each other over long distances by howling.

Like all dogs, wolves have an incredible sense of smell, and can detect prey, such as rabbits, by their scent more than a mile away. They can also hear sounds that are 6 miles away.

POLAR BEAR

Brown bears and polar bears are the world's largest land meat-eaters. Brown bears have a fearsome reputation, but they do not match polar bears' ruthless approach to hunting.

Polar bears eat most in the winter months, when they can hunt on the sea ice.

KILLER FACT
A polar bear needs to kill up to 75 seals every year to survive.

Polar bears are ferocious hunters. Their diet is mainly meat—from whales, dolphins, and seals. Few plants grow in the Arctic so, unlike other bears, they cannot feed on berries or fruits.

Polar bears can survive for up to eight months without food. They are great swimmers, and good sprinters. A bear may walk as far as 3,100 miles in just one year.

Seal Meal

To catch their favorite meal of seal, polar bears must wait by an ice hole, where seals pop up to breathe. A swipe with its massive claws and a snap of its jaws guarantees lunch.

Actual size!

12 in.

Huge feet help bears walk on snow and swim quickly.

KILLER WHALE

There is one predator that even a great white shark fears—the killer whale, or orca. These marine mammals are easy to spot, with their striking black and white markings.

KILLER FACT
Killer whales chase their prey at speed, reaching 35 mph, and even leap out of the air when they are in pursuit.

Teamwork

Killer whales often live and travel in groups called pods. They work as a team to catch their prey. Some pods just eat fish, while others prefer to hunt seals or other whales.

Killer whales are very daring in their hunting. Some even risk **beaching** themselves to snatch seals from the shoreline.

A killer whale tries to grab a sea lion from the beach. The whale must be very careful not to get stuck.

Killer whales are successful hunters because they have a range of hunting strategies and prey on many types of animals. Dolphins, whales, sharks, turtles, seals, and fish all have good reason to be afraid of killer whales!

While most bird species are not dangerous to humans, some winged creatures prey on animals much larger than themselves. Sharp bills, strong legs, and fierce territorial instincts combine to create some ferocious feathered predators.

GOLDEN EAGLE

The golden eagle is a huge bird of prey. It takes its name from its striking golden head of feathers. It uses its long, broad wings to soar and glide on currents, forming a "V" shape in the air. They often fly hundreds of miles while hunting for food.

Golden eagles have incredible sight. Their large eyes take up most of the space on their heads.

Perfect Predators

Golden eagles are terrific predators. They often hunt in pairs—where one eagle chases the prey to its partner. The **talons** on their feet kill and carry prey, while the beak is used for eating.

They eat everything from mice to tortoises, and even deer. Golden eagles sometimes eat **carrion** if live prey is scarce. After a feed, the golden eagle does not need another meal for several days.

A golden eagle spreads its huge wings as it lands.

Adult golden eagles are generally safe from natural predators, although their chicks are often eaten by wolverines and bears. Humans are the eagle's greatest enemy, illegally killing and poisoning these beautiful birds or robbing eagle nests.

Killer Fact

The Greek philosopher Aeschylus was supposedly killed by an eagle dropping a tortoise on him, mistaking his bald head for a rock!

SECRETARY BIRD

Raptors have curved bills, which they use to tear the flesh of their prey.

Birds of prey—raptors—are masters of the sky. Most of them have sharp talons, hooked bills, and huge wings that allow them to swoop through the skies looking for prey.

Secretary birds have long legs that allow them to run at high speed.

KILLER FACT
Secretary birds flap their wings when they attack a snake to draw its attention away from the bird's face.

Secretary birds take to the air during **courtship** as they look for a mate.

Secretary birds are raptors with a difference, because they rely on legs, not wings, to get around. Although they can fly, these birds spend most of their time on the ground. They walk through long grass searching for grasshoppers, frogs, lizards, tortoises, and even venomous snakes.

When the bird senses another animal, it stamps its feet to flush its prey out of the grass. As the animal tries to escape, the secretary bird chases it, stamping it to death with its large feet.

VULTURE

Vultures are birds with the worst of reputations, often seen as ugly, dirty scavengers. They feed off rotting animal carcasses, which actually helps to reduce the spread of disease by cleaning up this carrion or dead meat.

Love them or loathe them, their future is uncertain. Numbers have plummeted in the last decade and some vulture species are facing extinction. Food sources are getting more scarce and the birds are dying from eating poisoned cattle.

KILLER FACT

Vultures will fly incredible distances for a meal—one Ruppell's vulture travelled around 1,250 miles!

High Flyers

With an impressive wingspan, vultures soar high in the air to scan the plains for food. Some vultures can fly to heights well above Mount Everest, which stands at 29,029 ft. Most birds could not survive these heights, as there is not enough oxygen in the air.

Hooked beak for tearing at rotten meat.

Strong Stomachs

Vultures have incredibly strong stomachs. Their stomach acid can destroy bacteria that would prove deadly to many other species. When it comes to a kill, vultures are not polite. Fights often break out over who will get to eat the tastiest parts of a dead animal— eyeballs are a real treat! Some vultures, such as the bearded vulture, prefer to eat bones.

TOP 20 DEADLY FACTS

- Sharks can see in dark water, but they are probably color-blind.

- Spitting cobras blind their victims by spraying venom.

- Some prehistoric scorpions grew to lengths of 31.5 inches or more.

- Some experts believe a male chimp is even more dangerous than a male lion.

- One big meal is enough to keep some sharks alive for many months.

- Some prehistoric snakes were as long as a bus and as heavy as a car.

- The deadliest insects are microscopic bugs, such as bacteria, that cause serious sickness.

- Wolves will attack bison, which are more than 10 times larger than them.

- Sharks lose thousands of teeth over a lifetime, but new ones replace them.

- Horned lizards defend themselves by squirting blood from their eyes.

- There are an estimated 10,000,000,000,000,000 ants in the world, and most of them can bite or sting!

- A killer whale hits seals with its head or thumps them with its tail to kill them.

- There are nearly 400 different types of shark, but only about 12 of them are dangerous to humans.

- Some crocodiles can gallop, chasing their prey at up to 11 miles per hour.

- Bird-eating spiders shoot stinging hairs at their victims, causing intense pain.

- A polar bear can kill an adult walrus that is more than twice its size.

- The smallest shark in the world, the dwarf lanternshark, grows to just 7.8 inches long.

- About 2.5 million people are bitten by snakes every year.

- Funnel-web spider venom is deadly to humans and monkeys, but not to most other animals.

- Wolverines often steal the kills of smaller predators such as foxes.

GLOSSARY

alpha pair
A male and female pair that are the dominant animals in a group such as a pack of wolves.

ambush
A surprise attack made by an animal that has been lying hidden from view.

antivenom
A medicine that destroys deadly venom in a person's body.

bacteria
Microscopic living organisms—they can be dangerous and cause infection.

basking
Lying in a warm place, such as sunlight, in order to get warm.

batrachotoxin
An extremely potent poison produced by poison dart frogs. The frogs get the poison in their diet of beetles and insects.

beaching
When a sea animal, such as a whale, becomes stranded on land.

camouflage
A pattern of colors on an animal's body that hides it from predators or prey.

cannibals
Animals that eat others from the same species.

capybara
A large rodent that lives in the grasslands of South America.

carrion
The dead and decaying flesh of an animal. An important food source for scavengers.

cartilage
A strong, flexible fiber in animals' bodies. Sharks' skeletons are made from cartilage.

clotting
The process by which blood thickens after a wound has been made.

colony
A large group of animals living closely together.

constrictor
A kind of snake that kills its prey by squeezing it to death.

courtship
A series of rituals, such as flying displays, that animals perform to select a mate.

denticles
Hard scales on a shark's skin that help it to swim faster.

extinct
A species of animal that is no longer alive.

fangs
Long, pointed teeth that animals use for biting and tearing flesh.

freshwater
Water without salt in it, such as that found in lakes and rivers.

gills
Organs used by fish to breathe. The gills collect oxygen that is dissolved in the water.

girth
The distance around a body. The thicker its body, the bigger its girth.

gorge
To eat a huge amount of food at one time.

hosts
Animals that parasites such as mosquitoes feed on.

hatch
The breaking out of a baby animal from its egg.

invertebrates
Animals such as insects and spiders that do not have a backbone.

larvae
The young of animals such as insects, which change shape completely when they become adults.

marsupial
A kind of mammal, such as a kangaroo or a Tasmanian devil, that gives birth to very small young, which grow in a protective pouch in their mother's body.

mating
When a male and a female animal come together to reproduce.

nervous system
A network of nerve cells in an animal's body that carries signals to and from the brain.

paralyze
To stop a part of an animal's body from moving or feeling pain.

parasites
Animals or plants that feed on other animals or plants, called hosts. Parasites often cause their hosts harm.

plankton
Small animals and plants that float in the oceans, carried along by the ocean currents.

predators
Animals that hunt other animals to eat.

prey
Animals that are hunted by predators.

pride
The word used to describe a group of lions.

pup
The young of a shark.

radar
A system that uses radio waves to detect objects. The system gives off radio waves, then senses any waves that bounce back off objects in their way.

saliva
A liquid made inside an animal's mouth.

scavenger
An animal that feeds on dead animals or plants that it finds. Some sharks are scavengers.

segments
Parts of an animal's body that are similar to each other.

sensors
Organs in an animal that respond to stimuli such as light or magnetism.

serrations
A series of sharp points that make a saw-like cutting edge.

shed
To take off the outer layer of skin. Snakes shed their skin as they grow.

solitary
Living alone, away from other members of the same species.

species
A kind of animal or plant. Members of the same species are able to breed, producing young.

stalking
A method of hunting in which a predator follows its prey very quietly. When it gets up close to the prey, it attacks.

stealth
Moving carefully and quietly in order to sneak up on prey.

streamlined
A smooth shape that allows fluids such as water to flow easily around it.

stun
To knock an animal out suddenly.

suffocate
To die due to lack of oxygen, caused by not being able to breathe.

talons
The sharp claws of birds of prey.

tame
Not afraid of friendly humans.

toxins
Poisonous substances made in the bodies of some animals, which are used to attack other animals.

venom
A harmful substance that an animal injects into its victim's body by biting or stinging.

INDEX

allergies 88
alligator 60–61, 62–63
alligator snapping turtle 70–71
alpha pairs 122
Amazon River 40
ambush 55, 57, 69, 96, 113
ampullae of Lorenzini 11
anaconda 50–51
antivenom 49
ants 84–89
army ant 84–87
assassin bug 96–97
Australian redback spider 83

bacteria 92, 95, 135
barbels 10
barbs 91
basking 60
basking shark 8–9
bats 106–107
beaching 126
bearded vulture 135
bears 124–125
bees 90–91, 110, 88
beetles 87, 103
big cats 114–115, 118
bird-eating spider 80–81
birds of prey 130, 132
bites 31, 32, 33 59, 66, 67, 70, 81, 82, 87, 88, 97, 117
bivouacs 85
black caiman 56–57
black widow spider 82–83
blood clotting 92, 94
blood suckers 92, 93, 94, 96, 97, 106, 107
blue shark 31
boas 50
box jellyfish 38–39
bony fish 22
brown bear 124
brown recluse spider 78–79

bull shark 26–27
bulldog ant 88
bullet ant 89
burrows 45, 49, 58, 67, 76
butterfly fish 17

camouflage 23, 55, 100
cannibals 15, 19
carrion 131
cartilage 22
caterpillars 100–101
catshark 25
caudal fins 25
centipedes 103
Chagas disease 97
chimpanzee 112–113
claws 69, 99, 103
coastal sharks 12, 26
colonies 84, 85
colors, warning 48, 67, 73, 101
constrictor snakes 50–51
cooperative hunting 65, 113, 118, 123, 126
coral reefs 16, 17
coral snake 48–49
courtship 83, 133
crocodilians 56–57, 60–63, 64–65, 110
cubs 122

death roll 65
death stalker scorpion 98–99
dengue fever 95
denticles 23
diseases 92, 95, 96, 97, 134
dogfish 28
dorsal fins 25

eels 40–41
eggs 14, 15, 44, 45, 61, 79, 93
elapids 58–59
electric eel 40–41
electricity 11, 40, 41
emperor scorpion 99
enamel 23
endangered animals 19

extinction 19, 28, 56, 115, 134
eyes 12, 18, 30, 79, 103, 130
eyesight 12, 18, 27, 56, 88, 118

fangs 45, 57, 58, 59, 77, 78, 80, 81
feeding frenzy 87
fins 24, 25
fire ant 89
fish 8–19, 20–23, 24–29, 30–31, 36–37, 40–41
frilled shark 30
funnelweb spider 76–77

Gila monster 66–67
gills 9
golden eagle 130–131
golden poison dart frog 72
goliath bird-eating spider 80–81
gorge 115
great white shark 32–35
gray reef shark 16–17

hammerhead shark 18–19
hatch 57
hearing 123
heat-detecting pits 53
heat-sensing 95, 106
hissing 47, 54, 80
honey badger 110–111
honeyguide bird 111
hornets 91
hosts 94
howling 123
humans, attacks on 16, 28, 31, 47, 49, 52, 55, 56, 77, 78, 79, 83, 87, 88, 99, 101

imperial scorpion 98
invertebrates 102–103

jaws 37, 41, 63, 65, 84, 89, 117, 120, 121, 123
jumper ant 88–89

killer bee 90–91
killer whale 126–127
king cobra 46–47
kissing bug 97

Komodo dragon 68–69
kraits 45

larvae 93
lateral line 27
lemon shark 12–13, 14–15
leopard catshark 25
lion 118–119
lioness 119
live birth 14, 44, 51, 99, 109
lizards 48, 66–69, 80, 101, 133
longnose sawshark 10–11
lonomia 100–101
lure 71

magnetic sensors 12
malaria 95
mallethead shark 18
mamba 47
mammals 48, 53, 55, 56, 65, 67, 77, 94, 97, 107, 109, 115, 126
marsupials 109
mating 73, 77, 81, 82, 83
mermaid's purse 15
Mexican beaded lizard 67
milk 107
milk snake 48, 49
monkeys 77, 113, 115
Moray eel 41
mosquito 94–95
moths 100, 107
Mount Everest 135
muscles 11, 45, 49

nests 61, 85, 131
nostrils 18, 57

orca *see* killer whale

packs 122
paralysis tick 92–93
parasites 92, 94
pectoral fins 24
pedipalps 78
pincers 89, 98, 99
piranha 36–37
plankton 8, 9, 30
pods 126
poison arrow frog 73
poison dart frog 72–73
polar bear 124–125

possums 109
predators 14, 18, 20, 28, 30, 32, 39, 40, 43, 47, 48, 56, 57, 60, 67, 68, 70, 72, 73, 75, 78, 80, 84, 96, 99, 100, 101, 103, 106, 109, 110, 112, 114, 118, 119, 120, 122, 126, 128, 131
prey 8, 10, 11, 12, 17, 18, 19, 32, 33, 35, 37, 39, 40, 41, 45, 47, 50, 51, 59, 65, 67, 69, 73, 75, 77, 78, 79, 87, 88, 93, 95, 96, 97, 98, 99, 103, 106, 107, 111, 113, 114, 115, 117, 118, 119, 120, 123, 126, 127, 131, 132, 133
prides 118, 119
puff adder 54–55
pups 14, 15
pythons 50, 110

raptors 110, 132–133
rattlesnake 52–53, 82
remoras 13
reptiles 44–53, 54–71
rostrum 10
Ruppell's vulture 134

saltwater crocodile 64–65
saws 10, 11
scavengers 21, 109, 121, 134
scorpions 87, 98–99, 102
scutigera 102–103
sea snake 21, 44–45
sea wasp box jellyfish 38
seals 20, 125, 126
secretary bird 132–133
segments 103
shark cages 29
sharks 8–35
sharksuckers 13
shoals 36, 37
shortfin mako shark 24
Siberian tiger 115
skin shedding 45
skin trade 56, 60
smell, sense of 27, 56, 109, 118, 123
snakes 44–51, 54–55, 58–59, 110, 132, 133
social insects 85
solitary animals 16

speed 21, 24, 30, 35, 52, 53, 58, 59, 60, 65, 106, 114, 117, 125, 126, 132
spiders 76–83, 87, 96, 102
spines 100, 101
squid 10, 17, 21, 31
stalking 117, 118
stealth 64, 114
stingrays 21
stings 38, 88, 89, 91, 98, 99
streamlined body shape 24
swarms 90
swell shark 22–23
Sydney funnel-web spider 77

taipan 58–59
talons 131, 132
Tasmanian devil 108–109
teeth 10, 20, 33, 36, 37, 41, 65, 69, 107, 112
termite nests 113
territories 114
ticks 92–93
tiger 114–117
tiger shark 20–21
tongues 66, 55, 107
tool-makers 113
toxins 41, 72, 93, 96
turtles 20, 56, 63, 70–71

underwater breathing 9

vampire bat 106–107
venom 44, 45, 47, 49, 50, 58, 59, 66, 67, 69, 72, 77, 78, 79, 81, 82, 88, 91, 98, 99, 99, 100, 101, 103
vibration detectors 27
violin spider *see* brown recluse spider
vulture 134–135

wallabies 109
wasps 91
webs 79, 82
Western diamondback rattlesnake 53
whale shark 30–31
wings 107, 130, 132, 133, 135
wobbegong shark 23
wolf 122–123
wolverine 120–121

PICTURE CREDITS

Picture credits
(t=top, b=bottom, l=left, r=right, c=center, fc=front cover, bc=back cover)

Alamy: 28b WaterFrame, 30 blickwinkel, 30–31 Amazon-images, 34bl William Mullins, 52–53 Phil Degginger, 61t Allstar Picture Library, 64–65 David Fleetham, 88–89 Mark Conlin, 89br David Fleetham, 94–95 Wildlife GmbH, 98–99 Naturepix, 102–103 Stephen Frink Collection, 108–110 Gerry Pearce, 138–139 Alaska Stock;
Corbis: 2–3 & 114l Tom Brakefield, 56–57 W Perry Conway, 113 DLILLC, 115b Theo Allofs, 118–119 ML Sinibaldi, 120 Thomas Kitchin & Victoria Hurst/All Canada Photos;
Creative Commons: 92bl Bjorn Christian Torrissen;
Dreamstime: 110bl Yaireibovich;
FLPA: 15t D P Wilson, 20–21 Norbert Wu/Minden Pictures, 21b Reinhard Dirscherl, 22–23 Norbert Wu/Minden Pictures, 32b Mike Parry/Minden Pictures, 52–53 Pete Oxford/Minden Pictures, 96bl Piotr Naskrecki, 96–97 Chien Lee, 100–101 Thomas Marent, 101t Thomas Marent, 111br Peter Davey, 126bl Hiroya Minakuchi/Minden Pictures, 133tr Malcolm Schuyl;
Getty Images: 50–51 Pete Oxford, 64–65 AFP, 66–67 Visuals Unlimited, 78bl James H Robinson, 85r Mark Moffett, Inc./Michael Kern, 88 Mark Moffett, 89r Visuals Unlimited, Inc/Alex Wild, 99t Dorling Kindersley, 120–121 Robert Postma, 122bl Daniel J Cox, 123br Altrendo Nature;
Minibeast Wildlife: 76bl Alan Henderson;
Nature Picture Library: 4–5 Alex Mustard, 8b Alan James, 12–13 Alex Mustard, 13t David Fleetham, 14–15 Doug Perrine, 16–17 Doug Perrine, 17t Dan Burton, 23t Alex Hyde, 27b Doug Perrine, 28–29 Jeff Rotman, 36–37 Doug Perrine, 40b Alan James, 47b Michael D. Kern, 61b Barry Mansell, 67t Michael D Kern, 94–95 Martin Dohrn 97 Rod Williams, 106–107 Doug Perrine, 107t Dan Burton, 119br Inaki Relanzon, 122–123 Alex Mustard , 123t David Fleetham, 124–125 Jeff Rotman, 125r Andy Rouse, 127t Alex Hyde, 132–133 Joe McDonald, 133b Doug Perrine, 144 Alan James;

NHPA 9t Charles Hood, 18b, 18–19 Charles Hood, 30b, 32–33 Oceans Image/Photoshot/Saul Gonor, 46–47 E Hanumantha Rao, 48–49 Larry Ditto, 50b Martin Wendler, 53b Daniel Heuclin, 54–55 Daniel Heuclin, 55b Stephen Dalton, 58–59 Ken Griffiths, 59t Photoshot, 60–61 Mark Conlin, 65b Martin Harvey, 71t Image Quest 3D, 76–77 Ken Griffiths, 88–89 Dave Pinson, 92–93 ANT Photo Library, 93b Ken Griffiths, 102bl ANT Photo Library, 107b Daniel Hueclin, 109t Woodfall/Photoshot, 110–111 Nick Garbutt, 119t Martin Harvey, 124–125 Jordi Bas Casasj, 126–127 Gerard Lacz;
SeaPics.com: 11t Makoto Kubo/e-Photo;
Shutterstock: 6–7 frantisekhojdysz, 30–31 Rich Carey, 38–39 Vilainecrevette, 39t Daleen Loest, 39b R. Gino Santa Maria, 42–43 mrjo, 57t VladSer, 70–71 Ryan M. Bolton, 72–73 Klaus Ulrich Mueller, 73b Klaus Ulrich Mueller, 73t Fabio Maffei, 74–75 James C. Bartholomew, 79br F Duran, 99b Dennis W. Donohue, 104–105 Paula French, 114–115 dangdumrong, 128–129 2630ben, 130–131 & 131t Vladimir Kogan Michael, 130b Hanoi Photography, 134–135 Nadezda Murmakova, 135b Dennis Jacobsen, 135t Eduard Kyslynskyy;
SPL: 9b Gerald and Buff Corsi, Visuals Unlimited, Inc., 20b Geoff Kidd, 24t Andy Murch, Visuals Unlimited, Inc., 33b Andy Murch/Visuals Unlimited, Inc., 37t Visuals Unlimited, 44–45 Matthew Oldfield, 45b WK Fletcher, 49 Ken M Highfill, 57b Nature's Images, 65t Andy Murch/Visuals Unlimited, Inc., 65b Georgette Douwma, 69b Steve Gschmeissner, 80b Simon D Pollard, 80–81 Barbara Strnadova, 81c James H Robinson, 82b Steve Gschmeissner, 82–83 Nature's Images, 84–85 Sinclair Stammers, 90–91 Solvin Zankl, 91b Theirry Berrod, Mona Lisa Production, 94bl Susumu Nishinaga, 106–107 Tom McHugh, 107t Merlin Tuttle/Bat Conservation International, 125l John Shaw;